ANTS IN

Olivia Snowdrop

ISBN: 9798734151402

First printing edition 2022

Cover design by Olivia Snowdrop

This book is for you.

CONTENTS

*

In order for you to enjoy this book as safely as possible, I thought it best to provide some trigger warnings at the beginning. Please be mindful that the following topics are included: sexual assault/rape, self-harm and eating disorders, depression and – as the title alludes to – anxiety.

Look after yourself.

EGGS

ALL MY HEROES ARE UNMARRIED WOMEN IN THEIR THIRTIES

like single by choice. like child-free. like having many lovers but they don't really stick around. like space to breathe. women who need only themselves. women who are happy this way. who have time to write or watch the movie they like. women who walk to the cinema alone. women who make their home whatever the fuck they want it to be. women who know how to love but keep it for themselves. like we deserve that right? like why sleep beside another person when the whole bed to yourself is better? women who didn't crumble under the pressure to find someone to make them whole like who told you that? it's bullshit. women who decided the most important relationship is the one with yourself and stuck to it grew it and watered it you're a fern baby you're a tree. women i want to be. like teach me how not to want so much like show me shedding societal expectations. what's the right response to all their questions when they tell you you're gonna change your mind and you'll regret it like how is it anything less than a kick in the teeth? women who grieve the loss of your parents' dream but stay steadfast in your decision like teach me what it means to be so goddamn interesting.

there's a phantom in my basement called baby called child. tell me why i cry at birth stories and my arms cradle a ghost. maybe i just want the glow the attention the peace. maybe i wouldn't get any of these. my chest is an aching wound the way my unused womb is a casket. an antique. i'm not about to bring something unwanted into this world. but the tears. i am overwhelmed by the idea of motherhood. consumed, even, obsessed. it is everything i think about. it is daydream at best. it is, ultimately, a fruitless fruitless test.

when she decided to plant kid-shaped seeds and raise them stem to tip of leaf. was it conscious choice or unwritten rule that guided breath to budding lungs? these are questions she won't answer. did she think we would fix her? unnatural caregiver. little mistakes she has to live with. i told myself i'd never want this way never choose generational trauma. but lately i've been cradling a feeling warmth blooming beneath vacant womb. i dream of you at night unborn small gums and curled fingers clutching breast. why does my body yearn so? i do not know what it is to be a mother. is it this little one misplaced longing? i have resented motherhood all my life. it is a burden thrust upon us and i never once felt the pull. but i have confession *i have heard the call now.* i will not answer. sealing the chapter so there can be no intended inheritance of faulty framework. i will not settle just to satisfy an ancient contract that says being a woman means giving a life back.

HEREDITARY

the line between my grandad locking himself in the living room when we visit and me is a short one. i think it is obvious we share the same brain. my father's last name too carries illness along the tree and we three are the unfortunate who get the bulk of the suffering. glitches in the very bones of us. systems under loaded with serotonin with something like grief. i see myself as a child and i have never once not been hollow. emptiness is the only friend i've ever known. we make houses out of homes the way we flock to the darkness the way we shut out the light. we might not be made of human stuff. and i've had enough of passing poison down through generations. i'll stop the trauma train and leave the station swiftly. i'll take my faulty genes and go.

do you ever think about how you are literally your dad? how you walked a mile in other people's shoes but it was his that fit? do you think about it? how you inherited a sad brain a mad brain a brilliant one? do you notice? the pattern? the following a path. it's like, you didn't choose this, but here you are and you're on it now and you can't go back. you take after your dad. didn't they used to say that? you hadn't realised it was a warning. you hadn't realised they were telling you something you didn't yet understand. you're like your dad. you have the same eyes and you see the same way and most days you don't decide if that's special or devastating. lifestyle of the unemployed. lifestyle of the dreamers. lifestyle of my dad and me, not made for this universe.

LEMON KERR

this sour feeling like curdled milk in my stomach i felt this for you father. i had not yet begun to bite into bitter lemon taste acid on my tongue. and so i blamed it all on you father the resentment i harboured, exacting pain on a body that was supposedly mine. but it never was not when citrus fruit sizzled under the skin before i could even begin to call myself woman.

i got used to the anger of an absent musician instead of acknowledging the harm brewing behind chaotic walls. healing calls for remembering before forgiveness sets in. neither without sin you were upside down parents but you're trying father so i've heard. and now my brain is a lightbulb and i'm seeing things clearly. i'm seeing the lemon as well as the curd.

CLOCK FACE

i have my nan's two bottom teeth and my mother's tendency to laugh at her own jokes. i sit alone and cackle cackle cackle. when did i become this? oldest one in a line of witches. this burden itches like i have to repopulate the earth with my sweet nan's smile my mother's howl. i've let them down. i will be the last person alive with my particular face with this dna. no baby will ever look like me. no snowdrop small. i am scared of nothing at all except the concept of time and ageing. saving this specific reflection. linear direction. moving clocks. being unable to stop the needle from turning turning turning.

SWIMMING CERTIFICATE

every walk ends the same. the bridge is a test. i know
my final resting place well in advance. if i can stand in
the middle and stare at the water then maybe i'll stop
wanting to throw myself in it. it's not winning, when i
leave, dry. but then i never viewed surviving as much
of a feat, always wanted to leap, always thought i
should have jumped by now. my last bow will be a
swan dive, like learning to swim in a boy's school, like
looking back at my mother and whispering, *fuck you.*

LARVAE

waking to a window overlooking the sea, a tyre swing and tall devon trees. was i happy or did the salt always stick to my throat. did i choke as the sun melted like a fistful of butter coating the horizon. this memory is unwanted.

my sister hears a heavy boot stomping on a gravel driveway and we pretend it's just a dream. we pretend we don't psychoanalyse behind her back, wax poetic about mothers and the threat of them leaving. this was supposed to be unsealing.

light was meant to filter through. but you offer questions instead of answers, knock on the door of this place near the beach. on the cliff. can childhood live without tainting it black as hindsight. dusty coal. why does this holiday hold a knife to my neck and beg: examine the could-have-beens, scan for some sign, oh

there has never been joy. you were sad all the time.

ORANGE AND GUMMY OR NOTHING AT ALL

my mum buys me vitamins because she thinks i'm
going to die from some unspecified deficiency only
chewy medicine can cure. she thinks i'm going to fall
standing up like there are spots around my vision and
my legs are folded under and i don't know how to tell
her it won't be a lack of iron that kills me. she thinks
that she knows me. watched me weak and eating salads
a single ryvita in place of a meal. i'm not sure how i
feel. being constantly reminded of the sick girl i was.
i'd like her to trust to believe when i tell her that i am
all better just a blip in the line. i am just fine. though
it's hard to find reason to consume at all. this will be
how i fall. not from lack of trying. gentle slide into
dying. when it was too hard to get up and make
something to fucking eat.

DEPRESSION MEDLEY

my monochrome monotone mouth shrugs caring hands off the shoulders. discards kind remarks as a symptom of remorse. *how could she live this existence?* always bound to finish last. place is a nest where i lay my cotton head. coaxing joy from the cracks in my skin. i am desert girl dry, evaporated happiness. crust round the eye, sleepless socket. i am half of a human shell i am unwell. throat itching from the secrets i swallow. i am hollow *but you knew that.* i am detached, regarding roses as weapons. boxed in black and white thinking. without ink; it's just invisible words.

*I ONLY RAISE MY VOICE IN MY DREAMS, YOU
SEE*

you can't stitch a speech bubble over a waking mouth.
so in slumber i spout, my kettle boiling over, and these
lips are like parchment when i try to close them. the
spaces between teeth receive a wash from clean air and
tongue meets rogue hair, a side effect of breeze.

i am more than i seem, unzipping secrets, stepping off
cliffs that are called by their names. i do not holler in
vain; the ocean has heard me and is plotting retribution,
dividing invitations equally to the bottom of her bed.
and perhaps a liar dead will not heal cracks in my top
coat.

so i'll float on empty apologies that circle in sleep. they
do not follow me back to eyes opening and soaking in
shame is beginning to grate. every night i cannot wait
to jump into darkness. at least harm is acknowledged,
at least sorry is spoken. i'll take the token because at
least they are issued here.

at least i have that.

THERE IS NOTHING HERE FOR ME BUT AIR

it is june. there's an ambulance outside. i tell my sister i have a stomach ache and we get in the back. we are too young for this. we are both too young for this. one paramedic takes note of my wrists and quickly sits my sister up front instead so she won't see. they ask me why and i don't answer. i tell them about you. they say you're not worth it. it doesn't help.

i'm in a wheelchair at the hospital. it feels like a game. it feels like a play. we sit in a small room and wait. the calm before my mother finds out. the debris when she arrives. how it hurts that she's surprised. i nearly faint when they take my blood. the irony. i do not cry. i'm not sure i ever have. i think i might be an empty vessel. i think, i'll do it again.

pain, first and foremost. i was born into the wild unknown with the fresh sting of a scar on my wrist. you could unzip me head to toe. i was pink skin belly rising and falling into twenty thirteen. i boarded a plane and found myself in a dutch bar wondering why my best friend felt like hot water to the neck why my arms beckoned her closer and why the cold fear came to take her away. someone was drinking neon blue shots from a test tube. it could have been me. i crawled into the bad year. another new beginning and a view from the hospital ward. check these boxes and try again. i'm learning. now it's a university dorm room. i told charlotte that my head had never been the same since the incident. since the second undoing of me. we rented a house together and i threw up in an ice bucket. somehow i forgot blue drinks always make me sick.

ORANGE JUICE AND VODKA

you bought a round of sambuca shots on my eighteenth birthday and to be perfectly honest i should have known then. dangerous boy you look like a wolf in hindsight. what use is hindsight? packed in a tiny pub we're knees to knees and you ask me truth or dare. i flirt back like it's important. like you mean something. yes please to another round of vodka orange i'm getting good at this drinking thing newborn babe out the hospital she's ready for a fight. never have i ever and god i'm so heavy handed let you look me in the eye and i don't feel queasy not one bit. hindsight's a bitch. you lead me and i follow like i haven't got a clue where i am like man i shouldn't have drunk so much like home is so far away. you invite me to stay and it's disaster. i know what you're after, now. it's hindsight that hurts the most. i stand at the crossroads and choose your bed over a taxi. this is the place i trust to be safe. this is the place that is anything but.

I HAD A DREAM I SAW MY RAPIST IN THE SUPERMARKET

somewhere between the flowers and the get well soon cards. so i invited him to talk in the car park, promised not to cause a scene, just a quiet word as we stood in reflected neon. the sign above us reads holy ground. keeper of fresh produce. anyway, we're in the car park and he has a well-meaning look. his mum is there, fictional character, witness to a crime. he draws the line, we stand apart from her and i'm all reassuring, blame my period blame sensitivity, all these over-spilling feelings but i say i won't scream and mean it. start to cry and god aren't those tears a shout a plea, but i don't tell him that, just cover my face with my hand and blurt out the only thought that's been ringing in my head: *did you rape me?* there's a pause (i know the answer) but the silence goes on forever and then seven years more and when i open them i see the man i remember. his expression's contorted into a sneer or a grin and i can't take this in, can't process how this nice boy turned into the devil. so i'm running, i can't get away fast, and lastly there's his mother, the same laugh burned into my brain. she doesn't know my name but she knows her son and she loves him and that's reason enough, isn't it?

COCOON

FIRST KISS: 2010

i remember it like a film still: us, unmoving. standing nose to nose toes curling in ballet flats in the middle of an open plan park. not *the* park you understand but a childish version the sort of place first times occur. so we're here in view of the swing set and a slide i climbed in the not-distant past. and it happens. i don't think i see it clearly just know that you kiss me and i feel disappointed expected a firework to mark the occasion. if there's a reason i blame teen magazines and over-romanticisation or maybe dissociation that i couldn't yet name. it felt like i'd lost the game *you just lost the game* but i hadn't seen the future all the times you'd kiss me and the world would explode. and i suppose it's ironic (is that what i mean?) that ten years to the day i'd risk it all for that scene: your lips touching mine and it feels nothing like the first time.

but oh if you ever did. it would be like receiving roses after the high school play. it would be a snowy day and a text about my eyes. it would be guiding my lips to plant a kiss it would be this the riverside and a bottle of water. it would be slaughter.

it would be unravelling foundations that do not acknowledge the care. it would be unfair. we promised to never notice the small things that hold us like pink string folded around heart-shaped cookies. like tiny birthday cakes. like guitar picks. you mustn't ruin it.

(but oh please do)

I LOVE HIS BIG EGO
(after Beyoncé)

the way his mouth pulses and curves. talk about church
talk about worshipping something i want to reach over
and lick. the way he slits me open with his hands the
way he stands taller than me, protective. his restless
fingers and the places they settle. his whirring mind.
the way he finds silence and slips into it, comfortably,
forgetting every word except yes please this. god his
lips. the way his body curls. always towards me.
always gravitational. his soft pulling of palms to wrists
his planted kiss my neck a galaxy my bruises stars.
black hole landscape. badges of time. well spent,
always, with him.

i'm keeping a log of every time you say you love me and counting all the times you speak without words. like when you tell me i'm first in a list of people you want the best for and how modern language can't convey the way you feel about us. i'll make it obvious write the meaning behind phrases like when you tell me the places you're going to grace with your tongue. i'll be the one to take note of the number of moments you ponder if we were meant to belong. i don't believe in anyone but connection's connection and boy ours is better than most people find in their life. you're not mine but how we gravitate towards each other with pace how legs quicken to race beside you once more. and if the law of attraction is real then i pray that you feel my arms always reaching for you. and then you'll come back and we'll get to be golden. we'll get to say *of course* we'll get to say *i love you, too.*

CALL ME GOD

my favourite version of my name is the one that springs from your lips instinctively when the weight of wanting me pushes its way forward and you can't stop saying it: over and over, like making a wish on cake candles, you're murmuring into clasped hands at the altar of my body. and i hope you're not sorry when this is over

because shame is a catholic primary school and we didn't go there. do you ever think about where we picked up these habits? how we grab at bits of childhood and pull until the string strains? you can blame my parents for the way i pour energy into you. my safe place, cocoon. my open casket in an empty, church hall room.

DEAD FROGS

there's a dead frog at the front of the science classroom and it's time to dissect. we're beckoned forward but our bodies link. the teacher scolds us. i think arms folded around a person aren't as threatening as a scalpel. i think about how we've always been more interested in sex than death. yes we never shied away from being chastised didn't mind a wrong thing. but somewhere along the sin became comfortable the hot shame that burned at my neck dissipated and i became okay with the wrongness of it the once suffocating weight. secrets make for tantalising company and i actually sort of like it sometimes right? the thrill. i think you still need it too. the risk. i think we always did.

*PHONE CALLS BEFORE MIDNIGHT HAVE A
REPUTATION*

for being safe but i think we misplaced the rule book
on how to talk in code. you're writing an ode with
drunk thoughts and perhaps i should stall, stop you
from saying what comes next, but you left this
confession out like cold milk in the morning and i'm

learning, you can't jam words back into a mouth. how
do we back down from a feeling this large, how can we
close the pit we uncovered when we only have leaves.
do i wish to turn back time and plug up the whole sky?
you shouldn't have said it, sure, but neither should i.

BONE-WISH

my bones miss you which is to say you cracked my back in a park once and i haven't been the same since. i miss intimacy and the sound of knuckles against my ribcage. i think if you stripped me down to the skeleton i'd still have a body that skews toward you. my jaw clicks and chews and i spit out words like wishes. they sound like come back. my hands go slack without gripping yours for dear life. my spine is slightly bent meant to surrender. so when i miss you know it goes down to the marrow know it's not fragile know that the feeling persists. i'm asking for the gift of a cracked back in a park after dark near a supermarket i'm asking for you to remember it and do it again.

PHOEBE

i had a dream i saw a bed floating down the river and i think maybe it signals the end or maybe i'm just searching for meaning where i can grasp it. maybe it doesn't have to be a symbol it doesn't have to be the places we've shared washing out with the tide. it can just be a shiver a small shock of realisation a jolt in the direction of a change because i don't want you to float away i want you to stay i want the bed nailed to the floor not the ending. the river isn't our final resting place it's alive it's moving it's going somewhere. and i'm aware i'm thinking too much again and you don't like it when i do that don't want me to spiral my way out of something good

let rivers be rivers. let it just be a bed. let us just lie in it.

A POEM ABOUT CALIFORNIA BUT IT'S REALLY ABOUT YOU WHICH IS TO SAY IT'S REALLY ABOUT ME AND THE FEAR OF LOVE IN OTHER PLACES

god i'm so in love with california and the way the light bounces off the back of cars ahead. the edge of a block of seats in a movie theatre and wallflowers and heroes and windows. the next song that comes on the radio will be the soundtrack to our youth. i'm in love with the idea of a sushi restaurant and cheesecake bigger than my face. pancakes and the golden gate in san francisco. a new boy's shoulder in a mini van and feeling complete. god i'm so in love with california i cannot see it's a lie. cry about my appearance in a bathroom and try to ignore you ignoring me in this strange city in this strange town so far from home. you only love me when we're alone. when we're on the plane back to manchester. hovering in the air over the only place we exist. you only love me like this. here.

TOP FLOOR FLAT

in my dreams we're flooded in we're stuck here i see myself caught in a steel trap my legs begging to run. they tear at the seams skin fabric falling away. i have to stay. i have to stay. twenty six years later and i'm still in my hometown. twenty six years later and i still wait for your return. i cannot find it. i nest in grey of constant overcast sky. i am sure yours are blue. i am sure you have room to spread your arms wide and dance. i have none of that. only rooted. high in a tall tree with these eggs i each named you. no way out now but to fly. my chance is cut clean. you tape my wings to your own back when you leave. it's over for me. i will never see the yellow of a crisp burning sun. i could never get that close again to anyone.

I'LL CUT FLOWERS FOR YOU WHEN YOU DIE: SNOWDROPS, MINE

i'll tear the skin of this alabaster cold thing, pluck out the roots and call it sacrifice. my wilting leaves can be sheared, a meagre offering when the result is a girl grown from the mud. you may think me sturdy to break through the soil but i will spoil the surprise and warn you again:

i will be cutting snowdrops when you are dead.

and the weak thing, returns to the earth. the bell buds become pig food beside you, joined with the ground that always lay beneath feet. i will press my cheek to a gravestone, rest my eyelids before falling, down, deep into the depths of an overgrown cemetery, where we

once made out under the smoke-clouded moon.

METAMORPHOSIS

HOUSE PARTY TABLEAU

someone's eating cheerios in the kitchen, washing it down with raspberry shots. you take a picture of us, freeze the moment right before a quiet tragedy. i'm watching the spotify queue and sighing into a beer can. take the metal apart in my hands, feel good about an accidental incision. pretend it hurts more than it does. i feign love, kiss a boy i don't really like and stare into my phone screen. would you call me if you knew? i dance to mr brightside and forget i have the answer. you wouldn't.

I HAVE MORE PHOTOS WITH MY RAPIST THAN WITH YOU

we leave no clues no digital footprints we do not indicate that we exist at the same time. no body no crime. no evidence no case. i think you tell yourself this. i think it is probably comforting to realise it will end when i die. i do not find this a nice realisation. and it is unnerving for a person with an active imagination. like after all this time waiting i think i've concocted the whole thing. like did i bring the dead to life did i resurrect a memory am i reliving the plot of the movie ghost? there is not a shred of us. i wish it were you with your face smushed against mine because that's the kicker that's the real crime. the man in that photo hurt and he bruised and where are you? where is documentation of every gentle kiss and hand and lips and every moment you made me feel loved? you're telling me we've had ten years more *more* and neither of us thought to capture any of it on film? i know there is guilt here i know we're both culpable but it's not *that*. it's not that and it matters.

FRUIT BOWL

i slice myself more than i slice   fruit for eating and
peach skin   spits out strawberry juice.   i stare
down the noose, offer this arm as an appetiser, maybe
then you'd learn   to like the taste of secondhand pain.
i carve your name each time you leave   me and pray
the wound heals before you return, *god please come
back*.   i'd take a thumbtack   over a carving knife
but the effect is the same.   i'm still cutting fruit and
calling it shame; starvation is another word   for love
and anyway,   skin splits easier when it's covered in
fuzz.

your silence scares me, makes me anxious. you leave me and i cut lines in my skin. i think i can't swim without your hands on my body. i say i'm sorry over and over but it never really lands it never really sinks in. are you quiet from this sin, do you feel guilt like a belt buckle is it tight round your neck? i am unimpressed by the way the words stick to my tongue. i can't make a song from the screams in my head. do you want me dead? i know i would rather the end than have to face another minute alone. i think i made a home here under your touch and every time we've fucked it's felt like i actually exist. without this when you finally go i know i will kill myself but i can't say that because it's toxic so i don't and we both pretend it's not true.

that you'll never see. and i think about how you only get the good side of me the sheared version of this vessel the body that remains after i peel away the imperfections and present them as pretty present this as fact. i scrub myself in the bath i go heavy on mascara and you think that's just my face *it's not my face* i don't think you know how preoccupied i am with taking up space how inconvenient i feel i'm sorry if you ever catch a glimpse of my leg hair it's not my fault i was born a bush baby i've got incredible growth. you don't know about the boxes i keep trying to fit myself in i hate my chin how much is plastic surgery again why can't i be bare faced and brilliant like all the other girls? being wanted is a curse and it hurts because the person you desire isn't even me. i'm sorry: i don't think she ever has been.

MPDG #1

i hold all your secrets like pigeons' eggs delicate in my palm. if i squeeze from the arm down into fist i could definitely break this and that thought is satisfaction like the release of a breath. power is a test. you never asked for a pact but we've made one anyway silent agreements to shatter the truth. we cover up bruises and emotional aching.

if violence is shaking hands with a lie then you should tie me to the stake and burn the witch. i'm the bitch for keeping my mouth shut not the society that made me an impossible thing. i'm crunching on razor blades and trying not to crush you when it would be easier to spit them and learn to love the sight of blood.

LOVE AND OTHER BUGS

tell me what it's like to shake a body off like a bug. to flick your fingers at love and laugh at the fly. i think i'm the fly. tell me what it's like to shelter a feeling instead of shaking down doors and painting them blue. i think i'm the colour of you. i think i'm a fly with a paintbrush and i don't know how to drop it. tell me how to stop it how to shut down devotion tell me how you can run from emotion like it doesn't matter the sound in your head like you can't hear the pounding and you can't see the blood. tell me about your version of love. i think: it probably doesn't include me.

NECK DOWN NUDES

you told me once when we were young and more stupid
that i had a figure every girl would kill for and every
guy wants to fuck. something about that stuck. the part
where i am only valuable as currency. where my
existence is exchange. like great body, shame about
everything else. the personality. the face. i notice the
way that area goes without. internalised the lack of
compliment. learned to use my limbs to get things.
what an offering. a body. hierarchy i never agreed with.
now law. now dictating how worthy i feel. i still tell
this story. repeat it like a truth. you reinforced a thing i
suspect i always knew. this narrative stains my self
image and i cut myself in pieces, pose. share those
photos when i'm dead. nothing is more beautiful than
a girl without a head.

MPDG #2

i temporarily fall in love with every boy who's ever nice to me. it's a problem. i'm talking smiling in the street. i'm talking meeting for the first time and he doesn't hit me. it's a low bar. internalised misogyny's a bitch. is that an oxymoron? i was taught to be desired to be object to be seen. god i do it well. i'm the cool girl of your dreams. needs? i have none. i'm a fucking plastic barbie doll down there. but i think someone left me next to a fireplace. i can feel my coating melting away. so i don't stay. make me mystery make me villain i don't care. that's the point right there, isn't it? i'm not sure i've ever loved a man the way they told me to. i wouldn't know the feeling unless it hit me in the face.

girl brings a scarf to the station because i said i was cold. girl is older than me and owns things like multiple scarves. i own zero and just expect to freeze. girl's got me by the knees which is to say i'm smitten as she shows me the city in an alternate reality where i don't have to leave. girl isn't like me but i want her and i'm bold enough to say it. girl says she knew it. girl says i'm young and bright-eyed and we end the night in a bathroom where i ask if she wants me too. expect a non-answer. but girl gives me laughter tells me baby of course tells me *why wouldn't i?*

girl wants to date me. girl wants to take me out and show me how to snooker. girl wants to fuck me in the corner of a small town pub and i let her. girl hands me mulled wine and stands real close. girl doesn't care about my clothes. girl thinks femininity can be whatever. i like girl. she meets me at the train station. she doesn't care what people think. i think girl is special. baby aren't they all? girl wants to catch bowling at ten and kiss my neck at nine. girl isn't mine. but she could be. she could be.

PUPA

my skin has changed since that day. seven years and the cells are nearly done replacing. he will no longer have fingerprints stitched to my limbs. instead i have him and her and her and me and all the pleasures i chose for myself when i took my new skin off the shelf and decided to love this body of mine. there are still scars from the times i could not bear the burden of existing but i insisted on staying and stubborn is a family trait. i have had to wait for the trauma to settle under the surface to stop feeling worthless and to embrace the imperfection of healing unspeakable pain. but i have reclaimed my name. no longer just a thing you used to coax me out of comfort zones. i am making a home where entrance is asked for where consent is acknowledged. i'm not sorry! that it's taken a while to undo this. now anyone i let through this fortress will know it's a blessing and i'm a goddamn gift.

SELF LOVE AS A COMMAND

i love myself when i'm wearing sweatpants. i love myself when my hair is messy. i love myself when i stop performing femininity. i love myself. i like myself with period cramps. i like the spot on my chin. i like myself when i eat fried rice for the third day in a row and don't feel bad no not one bit. i love the way i won't commit to monogamy and can't pronounce it either. i love my dusty mirror. i like reciting my poetry in the shower i like thinking my words are some of the best in the universe. i like myself when the poems suck. i like myself a lot. i love myself doing deep breathing i love myself crying hard i love myself in the dark when i can't see my body whatsoever in warm weather with my stomach out in snow. if i say i love myself enough *i love myself!* will i like eventually believe it though?

SYLVIA PLATH

i regard pearls on the hillside, ripe for the   plucking
sheared and shedding second skin: it does not belong
to them.   these shells that stick like   tacks in
fields of grass   just waiting to be wanted, plump
enough to sink teeth into.   my body is sheep-like home
my body is not my own, no   something you can
take from   ripped fur   flesh or bones. my brain
is cotton wool coat   malleable lining cross stitch   my
brain is not to be trusted.   my shiny pearls are rusted.

PROMISES

dawn shoves me   awake.   i rise with the sun
but do not sleep   when the moon comes   want to
revel in majesty   magic sky.

if i ever leave   this place.   i will land at
ocean's edge with a promise   to follow lunar
reflections   down

to the belly of the sea.

EXHALEEXHALEEXHALE

i've always pondered the mountains   imagined
a life   of   sharp peaks. and i think it speaks to
the wind i was born under   wishing to move thunder
be anything other than   earth-bound.
so i wish to touch new ground   perhaps find
solace in fresh winter. after all   i have been sent here
with a cold flower's name.   the soil is not the same
as it was at first dawning. i'm looking for   oxygen
for   air   i can yawn in.

stand alone in a clearing. think about how life could end any second. make a mental note of all the directions you could run. this way over the bank and into the river. this way and it's back to the bridge. another and i'm running towards an abandoned freight container. will i find myself in an oil drum? there's a lone tyre here and i think about loss. i think about missing something you can never get back. i think about that. a lot. alone in a wide wide clearing and you are not here. i don't hear your voice i don't follow you. silent. i will either drown or swim. here i am. i am here i am here and i can sink or keep walking. walk all the way out into the lonely lonely sea.

FIGHT/FLIGHT/FREEZE

like biting into blackberry ice cream teeth first then
roof of mouth. cold hits the corners coating nerves in
my brain. freeze. like trying to stop time with tight
muscles. jaw and bulging eyes. squeezed. like lemons
like scrunched up brains work better. like sorbet.

my body is a shut down computer. remove the battery
and try again. maybe you'll get a response once this
virus leaves my system. like snow queen frozen like
glass jar trapped. your bullets don't hit when i am
suspended in space. when anxiety is a blank face.

PAREIDOLIA

there's an eye in the dresser. a sea in the carpet. i
haven't verified it yet but there's a bug on the wall.
spider foundations. cracks in the fabric of time. i find a
new face in every car headlight. almost always feel
chased. feel like running. duck my head below the
backseat. learn to get good at hiding. invisible stress. i
hurt my knee standing stock still and it looks like
crumpled baby. it is inner child. open mouth. my
bottom lip looks like chew toy and it is. it is.

MOON'S LIGHT

moon's light strokes my pillow head. demanding to be looked upon, thought about. she is glistening orb in jet black jacket sky. does she know i can't sleep without the office on? moon plucks clouds and makes them race. obscured for a second, she is brighter the thousandth time. moon shows herself in powder blues. springtime sky just reminds me of you. she laughs at my longing, earth-size perspective. regards my worries; they are ants in a jam jar. moon shakes rising panic from my bones. buzzing sternum stills; she makes me small in the best way.

THINGS I'M CURRENTLY MOURNING

my vacant womb. my body wanting something i will not give it. the empty ache like a hollow tree that nestles in my chest. the absence of this. of a child. i'm mourning miles between us. i'm mourning distance and time and circumstance. my younger self. giving love so freely. speaking it so loud. she was not afraid. the way you don't call me baby. not anymore. the way you used to. the way i didn't realise this until now. i'm mourning friends. i'm mourning old ones. my own inability to make them new again. the scars i carry go deeper than the skin. i am a limp thing. i'm mourning liveliness. teeth that fell out in a dream. the end of tv shows. little chapters shutting. the last time i'll ever kiss you. not knowing if it's happened yet. not wanting it to. you. you you you. us. where we'd be if i had just stopped longing. if i had looked around, grateful, for the beauty i already held in my palm. this poem. not knowing if i can end it. doing so anyway.

I'LL NEVER BE SIXTEEN AGAIN
(after dodie)

i think i was supposed to die a while ago. how else do you explain the way my brain stayed one age while my body is not the same body i had at sixteen. i'm closer to thirty than i've ever been. i'm not sure how to leave the past where it is. i keep dragging this suitcase to every new place i land. it's like i can't forget my old hands and the people they touched. i don't know why i'm stuck. when i was sixteen i saw black swan at the cinema. i kissed a boy after. i drank cider. when i was sixteen high school ended and i pretended to cry. i don't know why i did it. now i really miss it. i guess i don't know a good time until it's really gone.

REMEMBERED

most of life is just writing about death is just hurtling towards the end with force waiting for the way a body breaks not like snakeskin a slow slipping but rather a shatter this bloody matter falling away bones popping. i cannot stop it. my biggest fear is disappearing without a trace is waste is living a life so devoid of meaning that my guts are just guts and not a string of poems i leave behind. i want to find purpose but maybe this is it maybe it's just writing about breath like there's a limited supply because there is.

EXOSKELETON

THE FEELING NEVER STOPS

i killed two butterflies when i was eleven or maybe i wasn't who cares anyway i killed two butterflies when i was eleven by drowning them in water from a spray bottle with my step sibling and i didn't feel remorse. actually that's a lie i did feel something but only later when i realised what it was we had done. i drowned two butterflies when i was eleven and i could have been older but i just can't remember and isn't it shameful that a murder can be so insignificant but then again maybe it isn't because i still think about it to this day. yeah maybe i'm not okay, maybe those butterflies didn't deserve to die. we probably should have let them fly instead of condemning them to a watery grave because what good is taking the life of two mating butterflies if nothing is produced. a life for a life but not quite because we probably cut their chances off right at the climax and i'm sorry to those orgasms that never got to come. it's been one of those incidents i just can't get over and the guilt is a spray bottle to the brain every now and again it hits some nerve deep inside me and i'm knocked to my knees to pray to the sky that i don't get sent down for drowning two mating butterflies when i was probably eleven or maybe i wasn't who cares anyway

SYMPTOM

i'm going to put my fist through a wall. slam my hand into brick until the knuckles rip apart and i can see the bone, see that this home i inhabit is real, i exist here. i'm going to slam my head on the concrete, watch my thoughts roll out across the pavement, let someone else look at them, weep at them. i'm suffocating. i can feel it.

my heart is caving in on itself and i don't know how to stop it, don't know if i'm made of rocket fuel or just emotionally unstable. i'll place my eyes on the table, plucked straight from the skull, just so i don't have to look at myself, don't have to live in this museum much longer. i'm not strong for sewing my mouth shut. i think i'm a coward.

i think i might be afraid to say a fraction of the truth. i'm scared of you. every finger that taps a screen. who do you see, who do you think i am because i know it isn't me, it isn't the person who slips wordlessly around a room, makes this house a tomb and lies in it, dead quiet. dead still.

BEAUTIFUL SOUL BABE

i wake up and a girl on instagram calls me a goddess
tells me i have a beautiful soul. what doesn't she know?
she's got the secrets of the universe and she can see
right through me. apparently i'm meant to be here.
apparently i'm not a leech. she hasn't seen me suckling
on the breath of those i love. she hasn't known me
suffering through any lens without a filter. if i'm a
goddess i'm a bad one. i keep making dark things
happen. here's a photo of me with dead eyes but just
ignore that. maybe i rendered it to death. you don't
really know me yet. you haven't heard me screaming.
instagram girl you should know i'm half-pretending
you should know i'm half a lie. instagram girl tell me
why you think i'm beautiful when you're scrolling
through my page. can you not feel the rage? why'd you
call me babe? why'd you see me that way?

MY BODY IS A SCRATCHING POST, A PLACE FOR BLEEDING

and i have been deceiving: i wear my sleeves long so you cannot see how hard it is to live when you know you don't belong. it's wrong: how can i talk about healing when i'm dealing with fresh cuts on my wrists. when i'm trying to stem the misery that pours from me, all the missing you and wishing i was kissing, and hurting her and pretending i am not certain i deserve it i deserve it i deserve it

i think i am made for searing, made for the sting from the lemon in my veins. i inflict this pain as a way to plant my feet on concrete (as if it's easy as if all it takes is metal and flesh). what will be left of a woman who scores herself to death? soon i'll be nothing but a picture on a screen, and that is not even me! where are the red-lined arms, tell me, where are the scars?

DON'T CRY OVER SQUASHED MOTHS

weighted wrists wring glasses until they're close to
cracking. turn up the tap and let the water scald and
renew. learn to forget you, with every twist of the cloth.
i kill a moth, with wet fingers, and feel its small breath
leave with the last of my empathy. and it's a modern
tragedy

that i never could love, something that so easily returns
to dust. this kitchen sink drama, witnessing a sort of
grief. i wash each piece of squashed bug down the
drain. i don't give it a name. my wrists work the same,
wringing the plates. i let the big pots soak. don't
acknowledge the lump in my throat.

BLADE BABY

i am spikes   not softness not sweet syrup
honey-dipped sort of sponge-like girl   i am
razor-edge   too sharp   closeness makes me cut you
i hurt i burn i do not heal

this is how it feels   to be sword-girl   severe
not nice not   pretty just daggers   for fingers   silently
slicing   until   there's   nothing   left
to   ruin.

WHO REMEMBERS ANYTHING AFTER HIGH SCHOOL?

i don't remember amsterdam. or the way it felt to miss you in it. that trip spans the length of a needle in my brain and i feel it, small and silver, the point making just enough contact to remind me i've forgotten. will a memory turn rotten if you can't recall the year?

i have a black and white photo of graffiti and the smell of tuna from a can. maybe bran flakes too, dry. there's no milk in our hotel room. i float on a canal boat and avoid questions about appetite. we might see the famous attic but the line is too long.

i'm not the only one empty so i exercise in the lobby. in the wild, they call this dominance. to an eighteen year old girl, it is revenge.

THERE'S BLOOD ON MY HANDS—

i've killed so many bugs i don't recognise   myself
at all. never realised i contained   anger and rage
untethered   leads to little deaths. i am the ant.
the spider. the butterfly. soundlessly   leaving
this world. no trace of existence no evidence   of
a life lived   (w)hol(l)y.   i could disappear
tomorrow and no one would notice.   like
a fly clinging to brick   i am bound to the wall. like
wasps in car windows   i'm not welcome here at all.

MY BODY ON A SLAB OF MARBLE: A MARVEL OR JUST ANOTHER DEAD THING?

am i corpse or statue? i will either blink or stare. is it fair to say i've been cold my entire life? now i'm getting the knife, steel placed on sternum. i feel certain this unstitching won't take very long. if i were a swan then this blood might be graceful, might leave roses on tables instead of rust in your mouth. as it is, i'm a trout and my scales slip: silent thuds hitting the ground.

i may come round during this peeling but drained feelings don't make a dent so i'll be fine. you may sip on the wine my vessel provides but remember the poison that traces these limbs. do i taste of him? i think i'm more memory than presence so my present to the guzzlers is a puzzle to solve. did he love me or was i cold? was i dying or just exposed?

ACKNOWLEDGMENTS

SHEFF-MAN '20 was first published in the 'Love in Fragments' issue of Honeyfire Literary Magazine under the original title *THE TEMPLE*. I would like to thank Lauren for featuring me and giving my poem a beautiful home alongside so many talented writers.

By extension, I want to thank everyone who has been following my journey on Instagram, whether you were there from the beginning or have just now joined. None of this would be possible without the support I have over there, so many poets who I am in awe of every day. To my advanced readers - Lauren, Diane, Jasmine, Bri - thank you for giving me the confidence to move forward and for spending time with my words. Finally, to Kristiana: you've always been there. This book would not be here without you. I suspect I would not either. I will always be grateful my friend. Thank you.

To the other support systems: the therapists, the abolitionist organisers and educators who have taught me so much, Eleanor (my first and oldest bestie), the (still) long-suffering, dinner-making, idea-bouncing roommate/friend/*person,* Lauren B. Thank you doesn't cover it. You are solid as a rock.

Thank you to my sisters, Antonia and Jemima. I am proud of you every day. Watching you become who you are is the greatest *real* joy.

*

Last thanks to the people in this book. Maybe you know who you are and maybe you don't. Maybe we haven't spoken for years or maybe we still do. To you, in particular, I would like to say: I do not believe everything happens for a reason but everything happens. Everything happens and some of it is good. *Thank you for being good.*

ABOUT THE AUTHOR

Olivia Snowdrop is a twenty-seven year old from Manchester, UK. This is their second poetry collection. They self-published their first book, *Snowdrop: A Collection*, in 2020.

Olivia also posts her work regularly on social media and you can follow her on Instagram @oliviasnowdrop

Printed in Great Britain
by Amazon